MENTORSHIP:
A PATHWAY TO
CAREER SUCCESS

by

Rita S. Boags, Ph.D.

authorHOUSE®

AuthorHouse™
1663 Liberty Drive, Suite 200
Bloomington, IN 47403
www.authorhouse.com
Phone: 1-800-839-8640

First published by AuthorHouse 9/2/2008

ISBN: 978-1-4343-9715-7 (sc)

Library of Congress Control Number: 2008905660

Printed in the United States of America
Bloomington, Indiana

This book is printed on acid-free paper.

ACKNOWLEDGEMENTS

I have been a fortunate person to have so many teachers within my family and outside it. My parents provided me with a first class education in Catholic schools that were available in Watts, California. They had a vision of a prosperous and rewarding life for their children and held to it no matter what the odds or obstacles. They exposed me to many ways to succeed. From my father's wonderful music that he played in our living room with my esteemed uncle Omer Simeon, to my older brother who as a Tuskegee Airmen beat all of the odds and stereotypes held about African American men. All of my eight siblings – Albert, Arlene, Shirley, Omer, Lola, Richard, Ken and Steve got me started and keep me going. They are some of the most accomplished and loving people that I know - easily intertwining artistic capabilities, skilled craftsmanship, music, engineering and especially fun. The gumbo gatherings that move from house to house up and down the Pacific coast are ways that we connect with our past and continue our parents' legacy.

I especially want to thank my four children, Lisa, Martin, Sarah and Tina for all they have done for me in their support, love and honesty in our relationships. I revel in their accomplishments and their willingness to go to the next step and explore new and uncharted territory.

To my mentors, Drs. Charles Thomas and Price Cobbs and to organizations that invited me to speak and present: especially the International Mentoring Association, Pacific Management Systems, and the National Diversity Council I am especially **grateful**. To my mentees, proteges, students, workshop **attendees** and audiences everywhere I want to thank you **for help**ing me find myself as a person and encourage me **through** your acceptance and your challenges. A special **thanks to my** good friend, Nan, for nagging me for ten years to **start writing**. To my friend Deb, who pushed me to personalize **what** I had to say and include my own stories and challenges **in this** publication.

And finally, in loving memory to my nephew Tony Simeon; lover of Porsches, fixer of all things mechanical and wine connoisseur extraordinaire, I wish you were here to share these moments with me.

AUTHOR'S BIO

 Dr. Rita Boags is an organizational consultant and educator who founded Leadership Technologies in 1985. The firm's focus is to design and implement human-resource development programs that impact diverse populations. Its primary offerings include career and leadership development, mentoring, and strategic diversity planning.

Dr. Boags has designed programs for clients such as the World Bank; DuPont; Fannie Mae; Hughes Aircraft; TRW; ICI Americas; Morrison Restaurants; Dow Corning Corporation; Phillips Petroleum Company; General Motors Corporation Finance Group; the U.S. Department of Labor; Abbott Laboratories; Lawrence Livermore Laboratories; State Farm Insurance; Mazda North American Operations; the Coca-Cola Company; Ernst & Young, LLP; US Department of Defense – DFAS; Air Products and Chemicals Inc.; Quest Diagnostics; and the AES St. Louis Chapter of the Boeing Company.

She has addressed numerous professional organizations, including the Minority Corporate Counsel Association,

American Corporate Counsel Association, the Conference Board, Society of Human Resource Managers, International Mentoring Association, the Multicultural Foodservice and Hospitality Alliance, the Multicultural Development Council, the Boeing Global Diversity Summit, the Texas Diversity Conference, the California Diversity Council, and the Maynard Media Academy.

Her firm sponsors conferences and institutes on mentoring, and it played an instrumental role in the 1998 DuPont Mentoring Conference and the NIST 1999 Best Practices in Mentoring Conference. It also co-hosted the 2001/2002 Best Practices in Mentoring Conference (see agenda at *www.mentoringconferences.com*).

Dr. Boags has published in *The Cultural Diversity Sourcebook, The Cultural Diversity Fieldbook Supplement*, the MCCA's *Creating Pathways to Diversity* series, and *Diversity and the Law.* Private publications include *IMPLEMENTING A BEST PRACTICES MENTORING INITIATIVE: A Coordinator's Guide and Toolkit; MENTORING: Information Guide; THE MENTORING BRIDGE: A Self-Management Guide to Informal Mentoring Partnerships* and the training workbook and video, *MENTORING PARTNERSHIP WORKSHOPS,* and *Strategies for Building a Diverse Leadership Pipeline.*

For more information on mentoring, upcoming webinars, and workshops, visit *www.mentoringsummit.com.* Descriptions of the firm's programs and publications can be found at the Web site *www.leadershiptechnologies.com.* Contact Dr. Boags at 510.581.2946 and at *ritaboags@comcast.net.*

TABLE OF CONTENTS

SECTION 5 CREATING THE LINKS BETWEEN MENTOR AND MENTEE

SECTION 6. SPECIAL CHALLENGES TO MENTORING RELATIONSHIPS

SECTION 7 YOUR PATH FORWARD

SECTION 8 EPILOGUE

SECTION 9 APPENDIX

SECTION 10 RESOURCES

PREFACE

A Key to Growth

Constant growth is the key activity for today's successful employees, entrepreneurs, and companies. All have in common one sustaining fact: In order to stay competitive and become more successful, they will have to grow. A strategy that is available for everyone to manage his or her own growth is through mentorship, the process of sharing knowledge, experience, and know-how between two or more people. The person who is seeking guidance—the mentee or protege receives it from someone who has more knowledge than themselves—a mentor. The sharing of knowledge between the primary recipients of mentoring—the mentor and mentee—serves many purposes and has multiple benefits, which will be explored in this book. Twenty-plus years of experience in implementing mentoring programs and evaluating the results of thousands of mentoring participants has led me to several conclusions.

One of these conclusions is that many would-be participants of mentoring bypass, ignore, and avoid this special opportunity for learning, and therefore, miss the benefits they could have. Many desire to move forward in their careers, and yet don't know where to turn for guidance and consultation, when in fact they are surrounded by people who could help. On the opposite side, there are many seasoned employees and businesspeople who have accumulated years of knowledge and experience, yet hesitate to reach out and share that with others who need it. Once finding the right vehicle to share that wisdom, they do.

Learning and growing through mentoring is so much easier than most people think. At its core is an extended dialogue with another person who can either meet a need for your development and growth or who meets their need to share their experience and knowledge. Naturally, the right two people have to come together to enter into such a dialogue and sustain it to reach the full benefits.

What is mentoring like? Imagine an ongoing dialogue with someone who has a rich vein of knowledge and experience that is along the same path that you wish to travel. And that vein of knowledge is one you have identified as wanting and needing more information to enrich and enliven your present work experience or help you prepare for the next level in your career progression. This information is shared with you on a regular basis; you have questions that are answered and the person listens. This same person can explain the corporate structure or operations of your profession and translate the unwritten rules of these separate cultures. Imagine, too, that from time to time that same individual takes you along to meetings, conferences, or business trips.

This person has questions for you and is interested in your life and your opinions. As time progresses, your relationship with this person becomes a safe haven in which to explore "crazy" ideas and get encouragement for your out-of-the box thinking. Suppose you developed so much trust that you could confidentially discuss your most difficult challenges with peers, bosses, clients, and yes, even your children. You have someone to call when you've won a big contract or you get the promotion you've worked on so long. This person is as happy as you are — you celebrate together. And this is just the beginning. Such relationships can go on for many years, even decades.

Reaching this state of being in a mentoring relationship is not all sweetness and light. Sometimes it's truly tough to take the feedback that you need to break out of your rut or stop a behavior that keeps you from moving into more successful territory. The investment of your time and their time pays off. You, as a mentee, have acquired knowledge that you could not have received anywhere else. And your mentor has the pleasure of watching you grow and stretch and reach more of your potential. Being a mentor is itself a growth experience; because the best mentors are those who are in a constant quest for their own growth. As you progress through this book, you will see many examples of mentee and mentor growth.

This kind of knowledge exchange and connection between people can be multiplied many times over when mentoring is carried out within the workplace or a professional association. The accumulated benefits of many pairs of mentors and mentees sharing within an organization has prompted many companies, public agencies, and professional associations to implement formal mentoring programs.

Many of the program participants I have worked with over the years come to the introductory sessions with a vague notion about the concept of mentoring and mentorship. They frequently do not realize the tremendous possibilities that it offers. My belief is that if more knew about its true potential for their own growth, more would become involved in mentoring—and few would dismiss it as insignificant to their success. By contrast, for some categories of employees, mentoring is essential for learning the ropes, becoming visible to decision-makers, and getting needed sponsorship for higher-level positions.

What prompted me to write this book is to turn the spotlight on what many are missing in terms of personal and career growth. One might call this book a guide for those who truly want to be successful in any endeavor and need a searchlight to see mentorship as a resource that might have been overlooked. This book is for those who are willing to explore what may be a new method of learning outside the classroom or from books: Learning directly from another person. It is also a resource for those who don't need to be sold on the benefits of mentoring and yet want to know more about how to maximize their returns in terms of satisfaction and tangible benefits. This book is also for those who like the idea of mentoring and see others benefiting, but who have let their misconceptions and prevailing myths about mentorship become a barrier to their personal involvement.

Becoming Involved in Mentorship

Anyone desiring to become involved in the more traditional forms of mentorship has three primary options: a) the informal or spontaneous method; b) a formal program established by many companies and government agencies; and c) a hybrid method that takes the best features of the first two.

I have labeled this third form of mentorship *self-managed mentoring*. As I explain each of the formats in later sections, you will see the differences in each and see the benefits in all. An important place to start broadening your understanding of mentorship is to look at its origins. From that foundation, you may develop a deeper appreciation of why the process could be such a critical component of your career growth and personal development. There are also group forms of mentorship and mentoring over the Internet. The group forms will be explored in the Epilogue Section of this book.

1. The Origins of Mentorship

Many of you already know the story of the origin of the term *mentor:* It is derived from a figure in Greek mythology, a man named Mentor. Mentor's role as a teacher, coach, and guardian is told in the tales of Odysseus and his exploits. When Odysseus left his family to go to war, he left the care of his son Telemachus to his trusted guide and counselor, Mentor. When Odysseus returned from his battles and adventures, together he and Telemachus joined forces to take back the kingdom from those who were plotting to overthrow them. As the story goes, this collaboration was successful.

The ending to the story of Telemachus, Odysseus, and Mentor has direct application to today's workplace because of the need for multiple generations to work together in a more collaborative manner. In the 2005 report, *Managing the Mature Workforce,* the Conference Board identifies the four predominant generations currently in the workplace and their differing values, perspectives, and work styles. These generations must depart from their age-related silos and create dynamic dialogues to utilize the best from each.

Mentoring, then, has become synonymous with grooming an understudy to take over the reins of leadership. In a fascinating article that appeared in *BusinessWeek (LaVelle, 2004)* the grooming for the next generation of the chief executive at Quest Diagnostics Inc. was recounted as an example of meticulous succession planning and grooming. The article described how Kenneth W. Freeman, the former CEO groomed his replacement, Surya N. Mohapatra, for five years to achieve a smooth and successful transition. Such an example makes good sense particularly when a company is poised for growth and needs strong and wise leadership at the helm.

Examples of classical mentoring occur in many professions, especially where there is a need for the mentee or protege to become an individual practitioner. This is true in a wide range of professions, especially health care, music and the arts, and the skilled trades. Through my membership in a church in Oakland, I have watched a very powerful lesson in mentorship unfold before me. It has been quite extraordinary to watch this relationship as it has evolved between the senior minister and her associate. Clearly, the senior minister — Reverend Elouise — has been grooming her assistant — Reverend Andriette — to take her place. As I interviewed the pair for this book, I got much more detail from their perspectives of what was going on in the four year process of "passing the torch."

What I could see clearly from month to month was the gradual handoff of duties. They would sometimes deliver the sermons together, and when the senior minister went on vacation or a church conclave, the assistant would take over. I could sometimes sense the lack of acceptance within the church congregation when Reverend Elouise was away. As the transition process unfolded, they shared with the congregation some of their differences and heated discussions. They are alike in some ways (race and gender), but very different in teaching style and personality. One of the advantages they have, that may not be available to many of you, is the ability to work closely together. This close working relationship provided them the opportunity to observe and give feedback to one another. From time to time, I have had that same kind of opportunity with my mentors and mentees.

2. Is Mentorship Right for You?

In today's business and professional world, mentorship has gone beyond its traditional meaning-that of grooming an understudy to take over the realm. Yet the notion that mentoring means that and nothing else still prevails.

I have heard more than one person say, "I don't need a mentor because I am not concerned with moving up the career ladder. I'm not looking for a promotion." My comeback to statements like these is to ask individuals if they have learned everything that they could possibly know about their job, the organization, and its business practices. Are they fully satisfied with their assignments and career? As of yet, no one has responded to me with a resounding YES. So where could the mentorship process fit into your life? Take a look at this list of career issues and see if any of them fit your present work situation.

(a) Managing the here and now:

- Current job challenges — anything ranging from an increased workload to lengthening the commute time because the physical work location has changed
- Work-life balance
- Reducing conflicts and stress with other people, including your boss and co-workers
- Selling an idea or driving an initiative
- Hanging on and biding your time
- Feeling excluded
- Illness – personal or in the family
- Unhappiness with a performance evaluation, raise, or bonus
- Reaching a dead end; pigeonholed and unable to move

(b) Preparing to move to a new position, employer, or location:

- Completing education or obtaining degrees or certificates
- Next iteration or evolution of the work
- Being seen or becoming visible to decision-makers
- Getting into the leadership program
- Needing a sponsor
- Looking for a new employer

(c) Periods of Transition:

- Onboarding, as a new hire or part of an acquisition or merger, or relocation to another part of the company or agency
- New jobs and assignments
- Promotions or lateral moves
- Pending retirement or unemployment

This list is by no means complete. I am certain you can add to the list. Every item listed above has in some way been impacted positively by mentoring. As we move through the book, you will see examples from this list.

Why Mentorship Is so Important Now

Today's high-flex job market calls for an ever-changing set of skills and competencies at all levels of employment. Mergers, downsizing, re-engineering, cost-cutting, reductions, layoffs, outsourcing and early retirement demand new organizational structures and cultures. Flattened organizations create career ladders with no apparent rungs or wider rungs with many more people standing there with you. New markets and global business strategies require that successful employees stay on a constant quest for new skills to be competitive; in other words this new workforce needs to be *career-resilient*. In an article in the *Harvard Business Review,* Bob Waterman (1994) defined the skills and mindset needed by the "career-resilient workforce." He described them as a group of employees who were dedicated to the idea of continuous learning, ready to reinvent themselves and take ownership of their careers.

These words were never truer as we look at even more challenging trends emerging in the workplace. The pending talent shortfall resulting from the projected retirements of Baby Boomers will be an opportunity for advancement for those who are preparing themselves now. For a more thorough examination of these projections, review the article or webinar presentation, *Are You Ready for 2010?* (Boags, 2007).

The need for diversity at higher levels has created a greater push to deconstruct the *glass ceiling* and remove other barriers to succession. The attempts to destroy Affirmative Action programs mean that individuals stifled under the veil of exclusion will have to search for alternatives that they can put into place themselves. For a deeper examination on the subject of mentoring and inclusion, see the article *Mentoring: A Core Strategy for Inclusion and Equity* (Boags, 2005).

For many employees, the instability in the workplace results in a lack of connectivity to other employees and to the employing organization. Reports show that a lack of employee engagement is a major cause of lowered productivity and morale for a majority of employers. Two recent surveys have shown that less than 30 percent of the workforce is fully engaged in their work (Fornal & Sanchez, 2005). The lack of full engagement is seen as a cause for high levels of job dissatisfaction, turnover, lower employee loyalty, and decreased revenue. Mentorship is a means to re-connect people and re-engage employees by establishing ongoing dialogues between co-workers.

A great example of how engagement can change the level of satisfaction and quality of work occurred in a pharmaceuticals company.

The mentee, Mary, was a mid-level sales representative who disliked the level of detail that was required in the preparation of sales contracts to drug stores and other vendors. She found the process laborious and felt that the detail was unnecessary. Through her mentor, Frank, an attorney in the corporate counsel's office, she learned how important this aspect of the job was, especially in preventing problems when a customer's bill came due for the products that had been delivered. Through Frank's careful explanation of all of the ramifications of her work, Mary came to appreciate how important the detail was and eventually took greater pride in generating the sales contracts. She made extra efforts to insure the accuracy of the contracts before she sent them on for approval. Mary's satisfaction in her work shifted significantly and she was able to share what she had learned with her peers.

While the need for learning and development has never been greater, most of us feel overwhelmed by the amount of information that is available. How can an individual stay on top of the ever-changing environments, requirements, and demands of employment? Mentorship is one way, because it is within the capability of each individual to do something about the information that is requested, received, and applied. As an individual, whether mentee or mentor, you don't have to wait for anyone to start the process; you can start it yourself. It's a lot easier to participate in a mentoring partnership if your employer or professional association sponsors a mentoring program or you are in a profession, such as health care or the ministry, where that is the expected norm.

Through mentorship, employees can find information when they need it and create those much-needed relationships that lead to an inclusive workplace. Once a mentoring relationship has been established, mentoring partners feel free to engage in dialogue on an as-need basis. The answer to a unique question may be just a phone call away. The information that mentors have to share has been culled from years of practical learning, problem-solving and meeting new challenges. The information once shared with a mentee gives the mentee new options and approaches that have a focused application to the world of work and the ways that organizations operate. How much better this is than having to muddle through any number of solutions before coming up with the right approach. Clearly this is one way to learn, but is a much longer and messier learning curve that could be avoided.

As the worlds of work and the marketplace continue in a constant state of flux, individuals—now more than ever—need to be vigilant about their livelihood. Learning is a necessity because what you don't know will hurt you—and some of us don't know that we don't know.

SECTION 1.
THE GREAT ADVENTURE
OF NECESSITY

A. Learning Is a Great Adventure and a Journey

Adults learn differently from children. As adults, our retention of information that is not relevant to our immediate needs is low. Unless we can apply the information to a needed and critical situation, we tend to dismiss and forget it. Our learning is most rewarding when we can apply new information to solve a problem. These are the lessons of experience that tend to stick.

When we are mentored, we get to tap into someone else's life experiences and learn to follow a similar path, if that is appropriate, and avoid the mistakes and pitfalls they made. Learning through mentoring is an even greater journey because the path to learning moves and twists with the needs of the learner and the teacher. That does not mean that mentoring partners don't have structure, but just as a roadmap is an outline from one point to another, we can also take side trips and detours in mentoring dialogues.

B. *Three Avenues of Mentorship*

1. Informal Mentoring

There's always that handful of individuals who know how to maximize their returns in a mentoring partnership. These same few get picked for mentoring in those spontaneous or "natural" relationships that so many envy. These natural mentoring relationships are typically mentor-driven; in other words, the mentor sees promise in a particular employee and wants to help the individual mentee realize his or her potential. We should understand that this is a very natural process, and mentors who pick their mentees want to know that they are making a good investment of their time and energy.

It should not be surprising then that those who get picked also exhibit many of the same qualities and values of the mentor. Mentor and mentee may seem as if they are cut from the same cloth; they frequently mirror each other in terms of gender, race, social class, and educational achievement. So not surprisingly, spontaneous or natural mentoring across differences does not occur as often as between those who are more alike. Yet, spontaneous mentoring across race, gender, and ethnic lines of difference does occur if one of the parties makes the effort. This is particularly true if the mentee is seen by the potential mentor as a winner or keeper. These selected mentees model the unwritten criteria reflected in the *corporate image of success*. Such mentees signal that they possess the qualities, traits and characteristics desired by their organizations. They are typically designated as "high potential" and chosen for future leadership assignments.

In a study of lawyers in law firms and corporate counsel offices, the characteristics desired by mentors were stated as these:

> "The image they [mentees] projected included not only working hard and producing a high-quality work product, but also appearing confident and assertive. Mentors looked for lawyers who showed drive and ambition, were sociable and involved in office activities, and had work habits that were compatible with their own."
>
> (Abbott and Boags, 2003)

The study found that many women and minority lawyers were unaware of these expectations. This lack of knowledge about the expectations of potential mentors was seen as a key reason for the lowered occurrence of spontaneous mentoring across cultures within law firms. While this finding is based upon objective research in only one profession, there is every reason to believe that the same dynamics occur in every other profession and sectors of business, whether public or private.

Occasionally, I hear of an instance of an employee getting invited into a mentoring partnership and turning it down. When questioned about why they did this, the response is usually either "I didn't know what they wanted or what it meant" or "I am okay just like I am." The undercurrent of these responses is typically one of defensiveness. I can almost hear their inner voices saying, "If someone wants to mentor me, they must think something is wrong with me." Quite the contrary: If someone wants to invest time in you through mentoring, most likely (but not always) they see you as a *person of promise.*

2. Formal Mentoring — The Employer's Rationale

Companies, government agencies, and professional associations have started formalizing the mentorship process for a number of reasons:

a) To involve more people
b) To spread the wealth of knowledge beyond the usual informal and comfortable silos and into the global workplace; and
c) To make the recipients of mentoring a more diverse population.

Many formal programs are designed for the employees who are considered high-potential or who are on the succession plans of the organization. These organizations know that mentoring is a key tactic in grooming the next generation of leaders. Beyond that, it is a great way for an organization to enrich its workforce with little time away from job responsibilities, and the information transferred is tailored and individualized to the person's needs. It is both efficient and effective in transferring knowledge and building relationships, both for those who are being groomed as the next generation of leaders and for the general workforce.

There are a wide variety of mentoring programs. They vary greatly in terms of design, implementation and results. In a fairly even-handed review of program designs and outcome, an article that appeared in the *New York Times* (Garfinkel, 2004) provided results of a survey conducted for the book *Love 'Em or Lose 'Em (Kaye, 2002)*. This research reported that "Some 60 percent of Fortune 1,000 companies now have some sort of formal mentoring." The article went on to report that many of the programs were not producing the results intended by formal mentoring.

Another commentary was less kind. In an article entitled, "Most Mentoring Programs Stink, But Yours Doesn't Have To" the author (Boyle, 2005) took the whole arena of formal mentoring to task. One of the shortcomings of the article was the lack of credibility of the "experts" commenting on the state of formal mentoring. These sources are mentioned here because your company, organization, or association may have a program in the "stinker" category, and you might avoid becoming involved because your peers or other participants have a negative opinion of the program. For a quick check to see how your organization stacks up, review the webinar presentation, *Fixing the Ten Most Common Mistakes of Formal Mentoring Programs* (Boags, 2006).

Admittedly, some mentoring programs do suffer from a lack of adequate structure. Many of the professionals in charge of designing and implementing mentoring programs have good wishes and little experience in putting such programs together. Most programs start out as pilots, and through feedback and evaluation efforts, improve their design and implementation to yield more satisfactory results.

Let's be clear about one thing: Employers in the public, private, and non-profit sectors start mentoring programs because they desire a greater return on the intellectual assets of their employees. They know that through the growth of their employees, their company or organization will maintain a competitive edge—not to mention improved morale and retention rates. When one employee mentors another, it is an investment of the intellectual capital of the workforce. They are transplanting information and know-how from one source to another so that these informational assets will take root and expand. Such a grafting of intellectual capital is an investment that frequently pays off in big dividends for the sponsoring companies.

Here are a few examples of how mentoring pairs saved their companies money. One of my shining examples of the outcome of mentoring was through an executive mentoring program held by a premier medical diagnostics firm. Together the mentee/mentor pair saved their company more than 3 million dollars in contracts that would have been lost to a competitor. Talk about return on investment!

In another firm, a mentee went to her mentor to ask for advice on choosing a vendor to create some specialized software for a high-end project. The mentor already had software in his department that could be readily adapted to the mentee's project. The mentee not only saved the time and effort of searching for a vendor, she saved the $50,000 she had budgeted for the software development.

In another instance in a well-known food-services company, a mentee chose a peer to be her mentoring partner. Each was the head of a team, and the teams needed to improve their collaborative efforts. Based on the dialogues between the mentee/mentor pair, the teams began to understand one another's perspectives, gained greater respect for each other's timelines, and eventually began holding staff meetings together. While it is possible to compute the dollars saved by greater collaboration, it certainly made the work between the two teams much less stressful and more productive.

I would encourage anyone reading this book to investigate what is available within your organization and through your professional associations. Find out what your employer offers and, if you meet the criteria for participation, sign up — even if you have to wait. In the meantime, you can launch your own mentoring partnership by taking advantage of some of the resources suggested in this book.

Even employees participating in mentoring programs may need additional resources to help them capitalize on the potential benefits that a mentoring partnership can bring. Some of these issues and topics are addressed in the many books on mentoring and the numerous articles that are written in the human-resources and training journals. Anyone could search out and read the literature that is available if they were so inclined. Some of the mentoring literature often does not speak to the reader's unique issues, or the reader may not be able to translate the issues into a current life situation. Some of the information is inaccurate, written by good-hearted people with a deep passion for the subject matter and little expertise. This book might complement or supplement information provided by a corporate or organizational mentoring program.

Some excellent resources are available for those who are the coordinators and administrators of programs. For those interested in more information on starting and managing a formal mentoring program, see the references in *Implementing a Best Practices Mentoring Program: Coordinator's Guide and*

Toolkit (Boags, 2002). A Web search will also yield additional sources of information and guidance.

Suppose you work for an organization that does not offer a program that you can join. Or you are an individual practitioner or entrepreneur. I'll show you how to start a small-scale mentorship program and help it to grow, just as others have in their organizations. All you need is a lunch hour, a phone, a computer, a bulletin board, and some eager co-workers or professional colleagues.

3. Self-managed Mentoring – The Do-it-yourself Variety

There may be an excellent program available in your workplace, but you may not get chosen, meet the selection criteria, or otherwise find yourself on a lengthy waiting list. For others, there may be no program, or the one that is in place may not suit your needs. Sometimes programs fall by the wayside before you can participate. Unfortunately, too many programs lack staying power, especially if the primary driver of the initiative leaves or the program gets de-funded because priorities have changed. That's where this next form of mentoring can be of value by learning to do-it-yourself.

My experience says that many people who could benefit from mentorship do not become involved because of old myths or because they lack a strategy to successfully start and sustain a mentoring partnership. Namely, they don't know how to select, choose, and work with someone who could enrich their professional lives. For such individuals, my hope is that this book will open the door to mentorship. Whether you are a part of an informal mentoring relationship or a formal program, the option to get mentored or be a mentor is always open to you. Having knowledge about the process and knowing how to get the process started will make it much easier and increase the likelihood that mentoring will become a part of your lifelong learning and development strategy.

This is where the idea of self-managed mentoring comes in to play. With self-managed mentoring, you are in the driver's seat, whether you are a mentee or a mentor. You get to determine when and with whom you will set up a mentoring partnership. This is true also if you are self-employed, an entrepreneur, consultant, health-care professional, teacher, homemaker, etc. Learning is always at your disposal by tapping into the wisdom and expertise of a co-worker, next-door neighbor, family member, and a wide circle of other people in your life.

With this book as a starter and other resources, i.e. *The Mentoring Bridge: A Self-Management Guide to Informal Mentoring Partnerships* (Boags, 2003), any individual can empower him- or herself to select, choose, and work with a mentor or a mentee. There are some fundamental principles and keys to making that venture a success, and the reader will learn more of the fundamental step-by-step process in the mentioned guidebook.

With the addition of self-managed mentoring, an employer can provide a broader range of coverage for those who wish to be mentored. This form of mentoring is both a complement and a supplement to informal and formal mentoring programs currently being offered in the workplace.

SECTION 2.
PRODUCING RESULTS
THROUGH MENTORSHIP

A. Success through Development and Growth

Far too many people let a vague idea of mentorship and misconceptions about the process keep them away from a mentoring partnership. I want to address these misconceptions by helping the reader focus on what the real benefits of mentoring are—the development of your skills and capabilities, along with the development of a relationship that can expand your career options. The stories of successful mentoring partnerships will give you a better view of what I want to explain. What real people gained in terms of knowledge and experience will show you how powerful this process can be.

1. How a mentor uncovered hidden talents in his mentee

An Hispanic male in an IT department of his company was known as a somewhat introverted and soft-spoken person. He chose a mentor in his company's program who was a senior-level manager in another department. Through their dialogues, his mentor discovered that he was very bright, had many innovative ideas, and possessed a sharp wit and a delightful sense of humor. In fact, he said that sometimes his mentee's humor bordered on sarcasm. They discussed this tendency to perhaps overuse the humor and risk coming off as a "smart-ass" to the wrong people. During the mid-year evaluation checkpoint of his company's mentoring program, the mentor commented during a focus group, "I haven't heard his boss mention him before. He is really bright and should be put on our high-potentials list. Perhaps that's something that I can do."

2. *How a mentee laid the groundwork for honest dialogue*

As a part of a formal mentoring program targeted to minority and female mentees, each participant pair was required to set some ground rules for their partnership. Earl (not his real name) told his mentor from the start, "I want you to tell me anything I need to know. I feel I can be more successful in this company, but I don't know how I can improve. Don't hold back anything." His mentor, a white male and senior manager, took this to heart. He took the time to interview the other members of his financial-services team, and was able to give Earl the candid feedback that he was missing.

Through the ensuing dialogues with his mentor, Earl discovered that he could make some simple changes, like having dinner with his finance review teams, rather than eating alone or with friends when they were away on a client call. That simple act alone changed the way Earl's peers viewed him, and increased the amount of client information he had at his disposal, since his peers and project managers often shared much relevant information over dinner.

Why was this so important? It is very important, since one of the areas that frequently bedevils minority employees is the lack of candid feedback in their performance discussions and development dialogues. Where there is no feedback about one's performance or professional presence (Bixler, 1991), one can't improve or have the option to change.

Many of you might be wondering just what you could talk about with a mentor and how might it change your life. Especially in the way you go about your work and your way of being in the workplace. We believe that the vast majority of people strive to be competent at their jobs and in their professions. Experience has taught us that technical competence is not enough — success requires a range of other competencies. It requires knowledge of the so-called "soft skills" and the informal and unwritten rules of the organization's culture.

While we put a lot of focus on the broad range of information and knowledge that our mentoring pairs share, we should not lose sight of the importance of the relationships that successful pairs have established. Most of you reading this book will want to know what it takes to get to the place where there is enough trust so that candid dialogue, and especially feedback, can take place.

B. Realizing the Two-fold Objectives - Knowledge and Relationships

I want to quote an idea first stated by a colleague and primary champion of mentoring, Bob Brandt. Bob stated quite succinctly, "Mentorship involves a merging of the head and the heart—people exchanging knowledge in the context of a relationship. That's why I think mentoring is so profound." Here is Bob's story as a mentor in a formal program sponsored by the corporate branch of a global organization.

Bob Brandt and Bernie Scales both worked in a premier chemicals firm. Bob became Bernie's mentor as a part of a pilot program in the early '90s. Bob, a white male with almost twenty-five years' experience, was a senior member of the human resources staff, responsible for affirmative action and equal employment opportunity in his department. Bernie, an African American, had just been assigned to his duties in the human resources staff as a diversity consultant. His background was in chemistry, and he knew very little about the human resources field, except that it met one of his long-term career goals, to move out of the plant and the sales department and into the diversity arena. Unfortunately, he was assigned to report to a former peer who had no management experience and was struggling to learn her new role as well.

The match between Bob and Bernie was a lifesaver for Bernie, because he got the best of all possible benefits of mentorship. During their one-year formal partnership, Bernie learned much of the details and emerging technology of the department. Bernie relied heavily on Bob's experience base, as it kept him from making many of the mistakes that a novice HR consultant would be prone to make. Bob showed him how to promote his ideas to the right people and get support for the initiatives that he was accountable for. When the formal program ended and they could have gone their separate ways, Bernie and Bob kept their regular meeting schedule of monthly Friday-morning breakfasts. They continued this for years.

During the course of their meetings, Bob had knee surgery and was confined to a hospital. Bob was shocked and delighted when Bernie took the time to come and visit him. He was concerned and wanted to wish his mentor well. That's how strong the bond between them had developed. Bob says that he is ever thankful to Bernie for engaging him in honest and thoughtful dialogue around their differences in race and differences in perspectives on life and the workplace. Bob claims that their dialogues helped him not to assume that he "knew" some stuff, just because of his job title and function. Through Bernie's tutelage, the ability to always make inquiries has become second nature to him. Bob has carried this learning into his community activities.

Now fully retired, Bob mentors at-risk junior high school students and participates in the rape crisis hotline in his community. Bernie has an extremely active retirement career. He has a small consulting practice working with public service and non profit agencies in his community. He is continually asked by many to share his expertise on mentoring, employee resource groups and networking.

SECTION 3
BARRIERS TO SUCCESSFUL
MENTORING

A. *Expectations that Can't Be Realized*

Frequently when we talk about mentoring, it conjures up images of the ultimate benefit of mentoring—that of being groomed and sponsored for a high-level position and perhaps having someone in your corner to nurture and protect you against the uncertainties of corporate life. These expectations need clarification so that when these benefits are not immediately achieved, people don't turn away from the process. There is no greater barrier to dialogue than an unexpressed hidden agenda. The person tracks what they want to hear, attempts to steer the conversation in a certain direction, and looks for signs that what they want is or is not on its way. This blocks the learning process because the selective filter is too small and the gauge too narrow. It's like a prospector looking only for gold dust and missing the nuggets.

B. *My Mentor, Warts and All*

Most mentors have a vast storehouse of knowledge based upon experience in their industry, business, company, and profession. They tend to be ordinary in many ways, and are not supermen and -women. Sometimes I read descriptions of the ideal mentor, and it sounds like a cross between Mother Teresa and Mahatma Gandhi. These highly idealized descriptions endow acceptable mentors with incredible communication skills, generosity of time and spirit, and now even cultural competence. Naturally, these most desirable characteristics are in addition to being a respected member of the community and workplace, having knowledge and experience worth sharing with someone, and a willingness to commit time and energy to the growth and development of others. For the majority of mentors who enter into a mentoring partnership within an organization or association, their mentoring partnerships are taken on in addition to working at their regular jobs.

Contrary to the idealized descriptions of mentors, most of the mentors that I meet are ordinary people with a wide reservoir of wisdom, who are willing to invest time and energy in expanding someone else's life and career. Some of them may not be very good coaches nor the best communicators at the beginning of their mentoring partnership. In the same way that we get better with practice at any of our human endeavors, so do mentors. The best mentors are those who are learning themselves. Those who place a high value on learning will be open to the reciprocal lessons that a mentoring partnership will provide. Mentorship is a situation in which the mentor is a student as well. What many mentors report from their program experience is that their mentoring partnership became a forum for mutual development and a stimulus to gain more competence in their current role or profession.

Here is my short list of what a mentor needs in order to be effective at the beginning levels of mentoring.

1. Experience and expertise in a body of knowledge
2. The ability to communicate about that body of knowledge
3. The ability to listen to someone else speak about their goals, wishes, and obstacles
4. Commitment to be in the mentoring partnership and spend an appropriate amount of time with the mentee

At more advanced levels of mentorship, mentors need the ability to provide career counseling, feedback, coaching (when appropriate), and share problem-solving techniques. Many mentors are motivated to improve their own competencies. The mentoring process will highlight a need to improve their communication and coaching skills, and subsequently they enroll in additional courses and workshops. This is the best of all possible scenarios, where the learning is realized as reciprocal. If we wait for mentors to possess every skill and nuance that we could possibly wish for, we will have a very short list indeed from which to choose. I probably wouldn't make the cut either.

What do mentees need to bring to the party in order to create a successful partnership?

1. Desire to learn; which means being vulnerable and admitting a need to know

2. A development plan and career goals
3. Willingness to invest time in the partnership
4. A schedule that allows for development and may cut into one's own time or hours before or after work

In a 2003 study (Abbott and Boags) of mentoring in the legal profession, the participants provided data that led to this conclusive statement about what mentees needed to do to attract mentors. It is worth repeating here:

> Potential mentors want mentees who they perceive as smart, enthusiastic, hard-working, and receptive to help. You must demonstrate these traits to show the mentor that you are worth his or her investment of time and effort. Take the initiative, ask questions, show your desire to learn, and be open to direction and feedback. Offer something of benefit to the mentor (e.g., assistance on a work project or simply the eagerness to become a better lawyer). Because familiarity is important, find a way to interact often with a potential mentor. The most fruitful interactions are on business or client matters, but almost any activity is opportune if it allows you to prove, through your performance and commitment, that you "have what it takes." If occasions to work together are not immediately available, create opportunities for contact by offering to help on a legal matter or by inviting the potential mentor to lunch.
>
> (Abbott and Boags, 2003, P. 27)

The core message in this quote is that *mentees must be proactive about their development.* Those who seek will find and mentors will be attracted to them.

C. Fears that Limit Involvement

Some of the common fears and hidden concerns of mentees and mentors can block participation in a mentoring partnership and thwart the dialogue process. Listed below are a few of the common fears that mentees express.

Mentee Concerns:

1. Why would someone want to mentor me?

Yes, why indeed? For me, this question comes from a place of disempowerment. It sounds as if the speaker is saying, "I don't think I'm worth the time." Or perhaps the person is saying, "I don't want to make an investment in my career, and I don't care if any one else does either." If you don't think you're worth the time for someone in your workplace to invest in you, then others will likely pick up on that, and guess what? Not invest the time.

On a more philosophical note, people mentor others because it gives them joy to do so. They take pleasure in seeing others succeed and avoiding the pitfalls and mistakes that they themselves have already made. As you read through the book, you'll see even more reasons why mentors invest time and energy in passing on their knowledge.

2. General myths and misconceptions about mentoring

Among the many myths that hold mentees back are expectations that can't be realized. Those who are seeking immediate sponsorship for a promotion, special classes, better assignments, etc. get disappointed when it is not forthcoming. Or they believe that a mentor needs to be someone at a very high level, and turn down someone at a lower level who would be better suited for them, given their place along their career path. We need to keep reminding ourselves that the core fundamental benefit of mentorship is development. Without development that occurs in stages, there can be no sponsorship. Sponsorship is something that is earned and given when appropriate, and given at the discretion of the mentor.

3. Fear of information leaks

At its best, mentoring is a confidential relationship. The discussions between mentee and mentor are not to be shared with others. Agreeing to this may be more difficult if you are in an informal relationship or you are starting and managing this partnership on your own. The one instance of mentorship where you cannot expect confidentiality is in a mentoring relationship where one of the partners is the boss and the other a direct report. Confidentiality needs to be a part of every mentoring pair's groundrules. See the Appendix for the Mentoring Plan Summary Sheets.

4. I'm not comfortable with someone who doesn't look like (think like, act like, come from my homeland, who worships differently than) me

Yes, that's probably true for all of us initially. We all have a choice to stay where we are, and through circumstance, get pushed into contact with new people from different cultures or even different levels within our own organization. Another option is to become more comfortable by engaging in dialogue and conversation where we have some control. A mentoring dialogue could be that place where we can create a safe haven for exploration and learning of a more subtle nature. The work of reaching out beyond our comfort zones is ours. The biggest risk is giving in to our initial discomfort and letting that be our guide to a stagnant existence.

5. Lack of candor

Some employees agree to participate in a mentoring partnership but then miss the opportunity for their growth. They cannot reap the full benefits because they are too busy resisting the learning that is possible. They are caught up in a game of pretense about their knowledge and skills. In this I can speak from personal experience. When I was working with one of my most profound mentors, the lack of candor on my part dragged on the learning cycle for a much longer period and just made our dialogues more difficult. I am forever grateful that he didn't give up in frustration and let me die on the vine of my own ignorance.

From a mentor's point of view, there are just as many or more concerns and issues that can inhibit involvement in a mentoring partnership, particularly with mentees outside of their normal social comfort zone.

Mentor Concerns:

1. I might hurt the other's feelings if I'm honest

That's always a possibility. This fear is usually based on a desire to avoid the employee's (or mentee's) response to feedback that is unexpected or unwanted, yet necessary to bring an individual's performance in line with expectations. There are workshops and seminars galore to assist every supervisor and manager to learn the proper techniques of giving feedback, guidance, and coaching an employee to better performance. These same techniques apply to the mentoring experience as well. When learned and applied, these techniques can help the manager and mentor become more successful.

2. What about complaints and lawsuits?

To date, research of the legal literature has shown that no such actions have been won by a complainant for making mistakes or miscues in a mentoring partnership. Yet the fear of lawsuits and complaints is often cited as a reason not to mentor someone across differences — particularly across race and gender lines. However, there have been some grounds for lawsuits based upon the **lack of development** provided by organizations. In a news article (*NY Times,* April 25, 2007, C1) regarding a class action discrimination suit filed by women at Morgan-Stanley, it reported that one of the main contentions for the suit was how the women were trained differently than men at the firm. And a lack of mentoring for certain groups could certainly fall under the development umbrella.

3. I don't know how to talk to a woman, minority, engineer, chemist, or anyone outside our department, of a different educational level, social class, ability to communicate in the language, etc.

In one of our mentoring workshops, an executive secretary shared with the class a dilemma that she was having with a new recruit into their engineering department. It seems that this new recruit, an African-American female engineer, wanted to be mentored by the executive secretary. The executive secretary had thirty years' experience with the company, had worked in many other departments, and understood the culture and the unwritten rules of the department. The young engineer had relocated from a Southern state and was having difficulty with the new job, the company, and the relocation.

The executive secretary's position was, "I can't be her mentor; I'm not an engineer." The class responded with all of the things that she could do for a newcomer, particularly someone from the same ethnic and regional background. At the end of the "joint teaching" from the other workshop participants, she agreed to be the young woman's mentor for the next six months. She would turn out to be an incredible resource for retaining this valued employee.

4. I'm not comfortable

Since when did comfort become a prerequisite to learning and growth? Remember your first job, first big promotion, first child (if you are so blessed) or first trip abroad. These were new experiences, uncomfortable yet filled with the joy and excitement of obtaining something we desired. Discomfort may be the sign that we need to pursue these new experiences for our own growth. When we take them on and succeed over time, they will become commonplace and we will become comfortable, competent, and confident.

For those mentors who have only known mentoring in an informal format, formal mentoring programs may seem unworkable because it is a new paradigm. After participating, even with their doubts, many report that the formality added a degree of comfort to the process and they were motivated to add components of the formal program to their informal relationships. They first had to give the new process a fair try and see what results could be produced.

D. Lack of Understanding of the Process

Many people new to the concept of mentorship don't understand how people get developed through discussion, observation, questioning, brainstorming, problem-solving, and sharing experiences together. Here are two fundamental sets of principles governing mentorship. The first is called adult learning and the second is levels of involvement. Let's review the primary principles of adult learning and see how well mentorship fits these principles.

1. Principles of Adult Learning

a) Adults learn when they feel they need to learn. Busy people usually do not take time out to learn new things. Besides, we rely on our ready storehouse of banked knowledge to get us through the day and through our lives. Why change anything if it's working? Probably when we are pressed into a new learning mode, it is often because of a critical need to change something about our lives.

b) Adults learn by solving realistic problems. New learning is often times the result of a crisis brought about by an impending problem that was ignored. Example: I learned accounting techniques when the IRS decided to help me become a better business manager by extracting funds from my bank account when they were available.

c) Adults learn by doing. As adults, we have a need for immediate application of new information, a technique, etc. At what point do we start brushing up on our French or Spanish, etc.? Most likely, when we are preparing to take a trip to one of the places that speak the language.

d) Adults learn best in an informal environment frequently through discussion and collaboration with trusted others.

e) Adults learn by different methods. We grasp things through different modalities. Some of us like to reflect and others like to talk. Some of us learn better through a visual modality and others auditory.

f) Learning and skill-building takes place when there is an opportunity for practice, follow-up and review.

Mentoring is a perfect example of adult learning principles in action. Mentoring, unlike training workshops, puts a small bit of information on the mentee's intellectual plate so that only the most relevant portions are discussed at any one meeting. These small portions get repeated, nuanced, and explored during subsequent discussions. This learning accumulates because the person is not bombarded with too much information at any one time. The learning has time to be acquired, applied, tested, and adjusted. Retention is very high for information acquired in this way and more easily becomes a part of the person's experience.

These principles are mentioned here because many mentees and mentors feel that if a conflict of opionions and differences in perspectives show up during the course of their mentoring relationship that something is wrong. Usually thinking that something is wrong with the match. While that could be an explanation, it is more likely that it is a sign that more growth is necessary along a particular dimension – usually in the area of relationships. It is more important in the scheme of learning to look for causes in the here and now, rather than seek to disgard the mentoring relationship. A mentoring relationship is an opportunity for growth in many areas. Challenges that are not handled here within this context are sure to come back again somewhere else until they are handled.

2. The Mentoring Process - Levels of Involvement

Like all human interactions, mentoring relationships have different levels of involvement, from the casual to the very deep. Michael Zey was the first author to talk about these levels in his book, *The Mentor Connection* (1995). I believe this information is of great benefit, especially to the novice mentee or mentor, because it helps to bring the expectations of the mentoring relationship into perspective.

Below is a chart adapted from his work, outlining the roles of mentees and mentors at different levels of involvement.

LEVELS OF INVOLVEMENT	
LEVEL I	**Mentor as Teacher/ Tutor**
Mentor Role	✓ Shares professional, career history and relevant personal information ✓ Imparts a variety of organizational knowledge and occupational skills ✓ Divulges inside information as to job content and shares professional know-how ✓ Provides tips on corporate culture – how to understand and to navigate it successfully ✓ Explains corporate standards and norms of behavior ✓ Expands perspectives of the current role, level, and future
Mentee Role	✓ Shares professional career history and relevant personal information ✓ Generates and shares career goals ✓ Asks questions and makes inquiries ✓ Candidly explores development needs ✓ Works to attain technical and business concepts ✓ Establishes and manages critical relationships ✓ Obtains an organizational roadmap ✓ Develops a corporate image commensurate with own personal and cultural values ✓ Provides perspectives of his or her level, profession, culture, life situation, etc.

LEVEL II	Mentor as Counselor/Advisor
Mentor Role	✓ Provides career guidance and organizational roadmap ✓ Shares problem-solving techniques ✓ Helps build self-confidence ✓ Acts as a sounding board and troubleshooter ✓ Provides opportunities for shadow mentoring
Mentee Role	✓ Receives support ✓ Information on career advancement – path and how-to's ✓ Builds self-confidence ✓ Receives advice on career, family, and personal dilemmas ✓ Explores differences in culture, levels, perspectives in different business units

LEVEL III	**Mentor as Coach**
Mentor Role	✓ Provides feedback to the mentee on current behavior ✓ Assists in the interpretation of performance reviews ✓ Coaches mentee on specific behaviors to build strengths and/or reduce performance deficits ✓ Respects differences in style due to gender and cultural differences
Mentee Role	✓ Explores input honestly ✓ Works with mentor to implement feedback and coaching efforts where and when appropriate
LEVEL IV	**Mentor as Sponsor/Advocate**
Mentor Role	✓ Acts on behalf of the mentee for the purpose of career advancement ✓ Sponsors the mentee for higher-level positions, special assignments, classes, etc. ✓ A role that is not automatic — provided when and where appropriate ✓ Earned by the mentee
Mentee Role	✓ Works to implement career advisement where appropriate ✓ Works with mentor to establish positive professional presence ✓ Earns respect and support of the mentor

SECTION 4
FINDING THE RIGHT
MENTORING PARTNER

A. *The Place to Begin Is with Yourself*

The person who can best say what your career goals are is you yourself. Based upon a self-assessment of the development you need to master your present level and reach your career goals, you start the search process. There are two helpful tools in the Appendix section of this book: the Career Guidance Worksheets and the Mentoring Readiness Questionnaires. Fill these out and begin to create the primary leverage points for selecting a mentor or a mentee.

MENTEE PERSPECTIVE

Looking for a mentor is not something that is always conscious and deliberate. I have started mentoring relationships in a variety of ways. At times I was not looking for a mentor specifically – I was looking for a person who had information that I needed. I always found someone who could help me and occasionally a mentoring relationship would grow from that initial contact. At other times, I have been on a path of my own development; not seeking anyone with a specific kind of knowledge, and a mentor would appear even before I knew I needed one.

Such a series of events occurred when I began my under-graduate studies as a social science major. At the time, I was embarking on a totally different career path from my previous career as a chemist. I was attending the local state university part time while raising my two young children and running a household. I had a long-term goal of becoming a psychologist and thought I would be entering a Ph.D. program by the time my children completed grammar school. It was during this time while attending late afternoon and evening classes at California State University in Los Angeles, that I came in contact with a mentor who would set my timetable on its ear.

I attended this local urban university during the era of intense student involvement and the emergence of ethnic studies courses and departments. Along came a professor by the name of Dr. Charles Thomas – the only black professor in the psychology department. Dr. Thomas was clearly about the business of recruiting black and Hispanic students at the BA and master's levels to enter Ph.D. programs. He organized us into an action group and taught us how to find schools and get funding. More importantly, he helped us to re-shape our image of ourselves and create a new vision of the future. He gave us *feedforward* in addition to what many of us seek in feedback. Before his untimely death, he used his influence to spearhead the matriculation of more than two hundred black and brown students through a variety of Ph.D. programs. I have never forgotten the great gift he gave me. It was through his tutelage that I obtained a fellowship to attend graduate school, way before my timetable. I didn't think that I could do it, but he convinced me that I had the smarts and the family support. I just needed to organize my life so that I could excel at school and continue running a household.

This is one of the things that mentors do for their mentees and proteges. Dr. Thomas had a vision for me that stretched beyond my localized and limited thinking. He provided support and encouragement when things seemed too tough. I never realized until now how important it was for me to have his hand at my back, gently nudging me forward and never letting me turn around and quit.

I have another example of how finding a mentor started with a goal or vision of what I needed for my growth. A little more than five years ago, I decided that I needed a white male mentor, preferably a former or retired CEO. What I wanted was to get into the mindset of what it felt like to run a large company. I also wanted to know if they worry about being white in the same way that I worried (sometimes) about being black. I also must admit that at the time, I felt intimidated when talking to or presenting to the executive officers of a large company. I felt that a mentor who was a white male would help me to overcome this feeling. I met this particular mentor in a most unlikely place.

While co-hosting a mentoring conference with State Farm Insurance of California, a gentleman walked up to me and gave me his card. He said something like, "Call me when this is over and we can talk about other organizations that could use your services." About six months later, I called to talk to him about his offer. It turned out that he was a highly sought-after executive coach, and his specialty was career transitions.

Jeff has helped me to think more strategically about the future - with growing my business and creating an exit strategy. Our dialogues have also had another definite benefit; helping me to get in touch with my stereotypes about senior level leaders and overcome my hidden fears and intimidation of CEO's and executives.

MENTOR PERSPECTIVE

Being a mentor is very rewarding and it isn't always fun. Sometimes it's plain hard work. Of course it's fun when you are sharing some special piece of information and you can tell from the look on the mentee's face that you have struck home. Many of my client project leaders become mentees and sometimes proteges. Let me explain the difference.

To me, any person that I mentor is a mentee. A person that I mentor for the purpose of taking my place and eventually filling my role in my company is a protege. I know that many programs and people in programs use the terms interchangeably. I used to do that. Gradually, however, I began to see a distinction and think about these special mentees differently. I may invite them to come along on projects and learn through shadow mentoring – a process of actually following, observing and sometimes working side-by-side with the mentor. When the right time occurs, with the client's consent, they can substitute for me.

Because many mentees and mentors have common areas of professional interest, it's not unlikely that they will go to conferences together and sometimes make presentations together. There have been times when a potential mentee will approach me at a conference and ask to talk further. I am always willing to have that initial conversation. If I don't think I'm the right person, I will refer them to someone else.

B. *Key Ingredients for the Right Mentoring Partner*

Here are the three key ingredients which I believe make up the foundation of any successful mentoring partnership.

1. Compatibility in professional interests

If I have the right experience and expertise to match with a mentee's desire for learning, then it's probably a good starting point for a successful match. We have a lot to talk about. I can tell the mentee some key points about the consulting profession, and also about starting a consulting practice. I can share with them some of the mistakes that I have made and how to avoid them. We can share publications and articles, and discuss newsworthy problems that impact our careers. When a mentee has crossed over into the protege realm, they are then able to help me with my consulting and training projects. That becomes a great benefit to us both.

2. Chemistry

Knowing what I want in a mentee is a great help to me. The mentees that I have the greatest fun with are those who are probably most like me in educational attainment and energy. I like to work with mentees and proteges who are thirsty for knowledge and passionate about their work. I like people who take action and get things done. Most have advanced degrees in the social sciences, but some do not. I have mentored a fair number of graduate students.

I like to be able to learn from my mentees also. One of my proteges began as a client contact and eventually left the corporate world to start a national women's organization. She hosts a radio show every week on diversity issues in the workplace. This is something that I felt needed to be done for a long time. Another protege has written and published several books. Again, something that I had not yet accomplished and wanted to do for a long time. She became one of several persons who continually prodded me to put pen to paper and publish more.

Mentors and proteges can take great delight in the achievements of the other. This is a part of the reinforcement and reward for being in the partnership.

3. Logistics

Mentees and mentors need to make themselves available to one another. Whether the mentoring partner is a mentee, protege or mentor, mentoring takes time. It takes time to create the relationship and then stay in contact. Surprisingly, the mentoring discussions that take place as a part of a formal program don't require as much time as many think. We have seen great success with as little as two hours per month. As a relationship progresses, it takes less time. When the mentoring partnership is thriving, the partners typically elect to spend more time together. E-mails and cell phones make it much easier to have planned and ad hoc discussions.

There are times when mentoring partners may not be in the same city — they may be in a distance mentoring partnership. These partnerships can work and may take extra effort. Sometimes one of the partners will make it a priority to visit the other in their travels. A mentee in one of our programs made it a point to visit his mentor when he was on vacation at a city close to the mentor's. They wanted to have some "face time," since that is the ideal way of carrying out the mentoring dialogue.

Above all, mentoring partners need to keep their commitments to one another. Breaking appointments and not keeping the confidentiality of the mentoring discussion is a sure-fire way to destroy trust. Mentoring discussions need to be regular, even if both parties work together in close proximity. In a word, both partners need to make time for mentoring.

C. The Search

The search itself is a valuable exercise. In our most successful formal programs, mentees interview a short list of prospective mentors. This short list is generated with computer software that matches mentees with prospective mentors on a number of significant dimensions. Many of the mentees returned from their interviews stating that this had been a valuable exercise from the standpoint of having met new people, and opened new thoughts about career choices by talking to virtual strangers in their company. They stated that it was easier than they had thought, especially with the pre-interview training we provided.

Without some preliminary training and a strategy for approaching and finding a mentoring partner, it's a lot tougher for the vast majority of people. This prompted me to start the Mentoring Bridge Program, based upon the guide-book of the same name (Boags, 2004). It is an effort to provide every person with the know-how and tools to find their own mentoring partner when they need one.

Here are some tips for finding mentors outlined in the *Mentoring Bridge Guidebook.*

1. Who is doing my current job really well?
2. Who has the job that I want?
3. Who is in a profession that I desire for myself?
4. My boss or immediate manager
5. Someone inside my immediate functional or business area
6. Someone outside my immediate functional area
7. Professional associations, affinity groups, and employee networks
8. Work teams, especially those that are cross-functional and initiative teams
9. Meetings and conferences
10. Referrals from friends, family, peers, and colleagues

One person I coach from time to time regarding his career found a mentor in a unique way. Actually, his mother found the mentor before he was even thinking about it. The mother, an engineer in a high-tech company, became good friends with one of her co-workers. The co-worker's husband worked in another division, at a senior manager's level. After meeting him, the mother decided that this man would be a great mentor for her son. At the time, her son was struggling with whether to go back to school to finish his degree or continue working. She arranged for them to meet, and through his mentorship, saw her son graduate from college and eventually gain employment in the company where she worked. The mentor has since left the company and started his own business. The mentee is on track for becoming a director in his company for which he credits the mentor's advice and guidance. Eight years later, they still talk and visit with one another.

D. *Approach*

The direct approach for establishing a mentoring partnership is probably not the best idea. It can be a turnoff because mentoring means different things to different people. Both mentors and mentees have differing paradigms of mentorship. Some believe that only natural or spontaneous mentoring has value, and can't imagine starting up a mentoring partnership with a virtual stranger. Mentoring takes time and effort to carry off successfully. It is an investment of the mentor's time and energy. They want to know that their investment will be well-utilized. So I recommend that those who are seeking a mentor make an initial inquiry that takes a few sessions to gather the information you are seeking. From these initial sessions, you will be able to determine whether you want to go further and transition into a mentoring partnership.

When I approached one of my most influential mentors, it was to get the answers to several burning questions. How did he become so successful? Most importantly, how did he make the transition from the mental health field into corporate consulting? After the initial inquiry, many more questions followed. What I least expected was that I would be interviewed by this man, a very prominent diversity consultant. Just getting the first meeting was tough. He lived in another city, and trying to reach him by phone was not fruitful. I was told by his office that I would have to make arrangements to come up to Northern California and see him.

While that was not going to happen anytime soon, I did find out that he frequently came into the Los Angeles area, where I lived at the time. About six months after I made the calls, he started a consultation project in the same company where I was working on another project. Our client contact introduced us and we started the initial conversations that have lasted for two decades.

I am convinced that anyone can do the same. I identified a series of questions that I wanted answered. Next I identified the person whom I thought could give me the information I needed. Then I found ways to set up a dialogue. Eventually I ended up working for this mentor in what turned out to be one of my most inspiring and fruitful apprenticeships.

SECTION 5
CREATING THE LINKS
BETWEEN MENTOR
AND MENTEE

This section is an answer to a very common question: How do you establish a mentoring partnership with a virtual stranger? By virtual stranger I mean a person who works in your company or is a member of a professional or community organization and with whom you have only a passing acquaintance. In particular, how do you build trust in a mentoring partnership that has to be started from scratch?

A. Relevant Dialogue

One of the most important features of successful mentoring is relevant content of their mentoring discussions for both mentee and mentor to experience growth and feel energized. In addition to relevant discussions, there can also be meaningful activities or at least activities that both enjoy. Over the years, mentoring pairs have participated in activities that both found enjoyable; e.g., bike riding, fishing, golfing (of course), community service, and attending conferences together. Bernie and Bob (see p. 14) found that they both had a passion for community service. Bob introduced Bernie to the Rotary Club in their community, and both gained great value from this extension of their mentoring relationship. Bernie expanded his leadership skills into a broader arena, and both had more opportunities for their mentoring meetings. Bob gained by bringing more diversity into the club's membership and watched with great pride as Bernie took over the chairmanship of the program committee.

What makes up a relevant discussion? The content is based upon the development needs and career goals of the mentee and the mentor's experience and expertise brought to bear on the mentee's issues. Other content can be brought in from many sources, such as the discussion of the results of a leadership assessment, a performance appraisal, how to prepare for a new assignment or complete an application for graduate school. All these and more topics are grist for the mentoring mill. Here are some examples:

1) A male mentee in a law firm asked to be matched with a female mentor with a family. He and his wife were expecting a child and their plan was to share parenting duties while they both worked. He wanted the mentor's perspective on how to do this successfully. The first woman he approached, a partner in the firm, turned out to be a poor choice as a parenting example. She had decided to forego childbearing for her career. However, she turned out to be an excellent contact and referred the would-be mentee to several other women and men in the firm. He did find what he was looking for and continues to

use all of people he contacted as resources in his quest to balance his career and his family life.

2) A Baby Boomer eligible for retirement in three years applied for a position that had been open for a number of months. While the position was open, she assumed many of the project responsibilities which were at the next grade level up and would mean a promotion. The promotion was given to someone half her age and without the relevant qualifications and seniority with the company.

Convinced that many of the company's human resources practices had been violated, she called her mentor to seek his advice. Her initial instinct was to ask for an investigation on age discrimination and violation of promotion policies. He advised against taking this course of action and suggested that she wait while the new person had a chance to get adjusted to her new role. Her mentor nominated her for a more visible and demanding role as a member of a task team advising the division president on proposed innovations. She took the role on the task team and found a place where her experience and abilities were much appreciated.

3) A mentor nominated one of his long-term proteges for attendance to a limited-enrollment conference. He called repeatedly and prompted her to attend. She did, and it turned out to be a career-expanding experience. The protege, a private consultant, discovered that other consultants attending the conference were not dealing with some of the more

pressing issues of their profession. The experience gave her more energy and confidence to pursue new directions that were not as yet explored by her contemporaries.

B. Managing the Relationship - Starting and Sustaining

One of the tools most useful in starting and managing a mentoring partnership is a mentoring plan. Over the years, I have used a plan that consists of three basic parts:

1. A statement of goals and expectations
2. A discussion agenda
3. Ground rules for the partnership

In a formal mentoring program, it is expected that everyone participating in the program will complete a mentoring plan. In the variety of informal methods that exist, it may be more difficult to get a mentoring partner to commit to a formal agreement. Yet, it's good to have an idea of what needs to be included in a plan. As an example, take a look at the Mentoring Plan Summary worksheets presented in the Appendix.

Why is a mentoring plan a good idea? Preparing a mentoring plan is a good way for the mentoring partners to start their dialogue. The mentoring partners must of necessity discuss the mentee's needs and goals and the mentor's expertise and experience that shed some light on those initial discussions. Preparing a mentoring plan is also a good way for the partners to get to know each other and share both personal and professional information that will make the formation of a relationship much easier.

A helpful way to think of a mentoring plan is that it's a roadmap. It outlines the journey that you think you want to take and it also allows for side-trips along the way. In both formal and informal mentoring, it's a good idea to have a road map because time is usually limited and it helps the mentoring partners to stay on task. The document is also a means for the pair to decide such elementary things as who should set the schedule, when to meet and the best means of contact. Many partnerships have gone astray because it was unclear at the beginning which partner had the responsibility for scheduling and the discussion agenda.

A mentoring partnership is an agreement between two adults and ideally is the product of both partners. In successful partnerships both mentee and mentor are responsible for its success.

What to talk about?

This is another of those basic questions that particularly novice mentees ask. So let's start with why you wanted a mentor in the first place.

1. Your Career

From time to time we all have questions about some aspect of our careers. If you don't have a notion of where to go next, you can talk to a mentor and get help for designing a pathway into the future. If you have a career goal already established, then you talk about that. What does that next level entail? What are the duties? How do you prepare? Should you complete your degree or take a lateral transfer?

One way to help organize your thoughts about your career is to complete the Career Guidance Worksheets in Appendix A of this book.

How do you make a transition from one career to another? I have made several major transitions in my overall work life, and I have helped others do the same. Suppose you have already been promoted and made the transition from independent contributor to supervising others and have no clue what is required of you. A seasoned mentor can be an incredible asset here. See *Monday Morning Leadership* (Cottrell, 2002) for the dialogue of mentoring sessions with a mentee new to the role of manager.

The use of mentoring to back-fill skills is a practice that is not used as often as it could be. Such a practice would go a long way to reduce the stress of taking over a position without some prior preparation. It will also reduce the time it takes to learn the new role and reduce the number of mistakes.

2. *Your development needs*

Everyone has a notion of what they might need to improve on. When you set a goal to move forward out of your present level or position, you immediately create a gap in your capabilities, so you need to acquire new knowledge, skills, abilities, etc. Can your mentor shed some light on how you can fill the gaps in your capabilities? What information has been pointed out to you through performance evaluations and other assessment techniques? These need to be discussed as a part of your mentoring dialogue.

3. *What's happening right now in the workplace*

Frequently mentees will bring to the mentoring discussions problems and challenges that plague them. A not-so-surprising number have difficulties with their bosses. A recent study by a Florida university reported that upward of 40 percent of employees surveyed had bosses who were disruptive to their work life (Ray, 2006). Other mentees may have challenges with their peers. Having a mentor to discuss these challenges within the safe haven of a confidential relationship allows for the candid discussion of difficulties and the exploration of options for resolution. At times it is just helpful to have someone listen and act as a sounding board.

Many employees want to make greater sense of their performance appraisal and get ideas on how to follow up or improve upon their ratings. In a recent onsite visit with a client, my contact shared with me her confusion over her most recent appraisal. Her immediate manager had made a conclusive statement at the end of the appraisal session. The statement, "there was no place left for her to move in the organization," left her confused and wondering if this was a negative or positive comment. The next level up was the position currently occupied by her boss, the VP of human resources, who had no plans of leaving, moving up, or moving to another executive position.

My client and I discussed what she could do within the company. I had long felt that she was underemployed and needed to set her sights beyond her present level and begin a career path that would lead her into the C-suite. She couldn't see how this was to be done, as a single parent with two children. Within a year, she left the company and became the CEO of a newly formed and highly successful women's organization that sponsors workshops and online training.

4. Quality of work life issues

There are many issues which impact the quality of work life and the performance of employees. Family issues, both in terms of child-rearing and elder care, can cause pressure and stress to both married and single people. Simply scheduling all of the responsibilities can take its toll. Extensive travel and increasing obligations cut into down time; some managers may feel obligated to answer e-mail late into the night. Working offsite at home has its challenges as well.

5. What's happening within the partnership

This is a frequently overlooked area of dialogue. In one of the case studies used in our Mentoring Partnerships Workshop, the mentoring pair runs into a major communication difficulty. In the case study, "Genetha and Robert," the pair confuses their expectations and arrangements for a future meeting. The mentee expects the mentor to participate in a banquet, and the mentor — a shy person — decided not to go, and did not tell the mentee. There was disappointment and eventual embarrassment on both sides. As a part of the case study lesson, the class participants discuss the sources of the pair's miscommunication and how the pair can get back on track and re-establish their trust. This case study is an example of ways that challenges in the mentoring partnership and the evolving relationship can be used as opportunities for growth.

Really there is no limit to what the content of the mentoring discussions can be. When it comes to content, the mentoring partners set the scope, boundaries, and limitations of their dialogue.

C. *Building Trust*

We build trust in a mentoring partnership in the same way that we do it in any other adult-to-adult relationship, a little bit at a time. We gather data about the other person and eventually form a conclusion about the person as to whether we can trust them or not. Why is trust so important in a mentoring partnership? Because, if we truly want this relationship to be a safe haven, then confidentiality of our discussions must be maintained. We don't want our innermost thoughts divulged to anyone, whether we are a mentee or a mentor. Information that is shared outside of the mentoring dialogue can sometimes be damaging because it can be taken out of context. There are exceptions to the rule of confidentiality. If issues regarding discrimination, harrassment, or violation of company policies are discussed, then uusally the mentor must report these incidences to the appropriate authorities.

From time to time, mentors are asked their opinion of the mentee. This happens particularly if another manager wants to offer the mentee a new position or another assignment. My recommendation when that happens is that the mentor and mentee discuss the request so that they are in agreement about how to formulate an answer. This recommendation is not always followed, and so far the results seem to be extremely positive since the majority of mentors want their mentees to be seen in the best possible light.

Since mentoring in the workplace is different from our normal dialogues with co-workers, the trust that must be earned takes on a different timbre. Here are some recommendations for building trust taken from the *Mentoring Partnership Workshop* (Boags, 2005).

- Commitment to the confidentiality of discussions
- Learning about the partner's professional and personal life
- Speaking and acting with consistency
- Understanding faults without exploiting them
- Learning to value the difference in perspective and seeking to learn from it
- Avoiding public criticism of your partner
- Inquiring about unknowns rather than relying on assumptions

D. Moving On

Mentee/mentor relationships do end. In today's environments, there are frequent personal or organizational changes that can cause the dissolution of a partnership.

1. Completions

Mentoring partnerships don't have to last for years and years, although many of them do. There could be a natural ending to your meetings and discussions because you have extracted all of the information you can use at this time. I believe that we need to always keep the doors open and be careful not to burn bridges when we wish to exit a mentoring relationship.

Some long-term relationships, those lasting more than two years, result in transitions. The mentoring partnership first went through the initial phase of getting to know one another, and gradually evolved into another phase where the exchanges deepened and the dialogues had a more profound impact. Eventually, as mentoring relationships mature, the meetings are less frequent and the mentoring pair may no longer consider themselves as mentor and mentee, but as peers. This evolution is a part of the natural process of mentorship.

There are other times that one or both partners want to stop being in a mentoring relationship or they no longer want to continue with this particular partner. In formal programs, we can invoke the "no-fault divorce." This process enables the partners to dissolve their partnership without guilt or blame. Typically we suggest that the mentoring partners include that in their mentoring plan at the very beginning. This gives either person the right to discontinue at any time for any reason. Any kind of dissolution needs to be done respectfully and with an ending dialogue that speaks to all the gains that have been made throughout the process.

2. *Loss of the partner through organizational changes – downsizing, retirements, relocation, illness and death*

These latter occurrences are a fact of today's workplace. All of these events can occur at any time. Added to that short list are maternity and paternity leaves, and anything that drains an individual's time and energy. Retirement or relocation doesn't have to be the end of a partnership. Take note of the longevity of Bernie and Bob as a mentoring pair.

If you are in a program and lose a mentoring partner, find another one; especially if you are just beginning to see the value of the process. Many programs make allowances for re-matches.

SECTION 6.
SPECIAL CHALLENGES TO MENTORING RELATIONSHIPS

A. *Incompatibility*

This is an unhappy state for any mentoring pair. This state usually develops when a mentee and a mentor are matched using an untested or poorly constructed set of parameters. Some mentoring program coordinators believe that a good match can be made on "style"; others match on "personality dynamics." What we have found over the last two decades is that there are five key parameters of matching that will yield very high success outcomes. Successful matching is a result of using both objective and subjective data in a reliable and proven process.

The best matches in our formal programs are based on these following parameters as outlined in the *MENTORING: Information Guide* (Boags, 2002).

1. The needs and goals of the mentee are matched with the expertise and experience of the mentor
2. Diversity between the mentor and mentee

3. Areas of commonality, including hobbies, community activities, volunteer and professional interests

4. Logistics, which include having a mentor outside the mentee's line of reporting, travel requirements, geographic compatibility, etc.

5. Chemistry between the two people helps the partnership "click" and makes it easier to get the relationship off the ground.

Even the most carefully engineered matches can result in an unhappy partnership if the mentoring pair does not follow through with their commitments. These broken pairs are typically the result of dissatisfaction due to irrelevant discussion content, lack of scheduling and missing their appointments to meet. The whole process boils down to a fundamental set of facts. If the pairs don't meet, there can be no development. If they meet and get no value from their meetings or the mentee is not receiving the information that is pertinent to his or her career, then the pair is likely to dissolve because there is not enough motivation to keep them together.

The input of both mentor and mentee is the key to good matching. Objective data based upon computer-generated protocols can narrow a search for a mentee. An interview by the mentee or consent to the match by both parties provides the subjective component. Visit the Web site *www.mentoringanalysis.com* to get more information on how this is done.

B. Cross-cultural and Cross-gender Matches

Mentoring across lines of difference is not as big a hurdle as many people think it is. Even mentoring pairs formed with persons from races and cultures with a long history of strife can be successful. Most of these pairs need a way to have some of their fears and concerns addressed early on, so that these do not become a barrier to their mentoring dialogues. The concerns we bring into a mentoring partnership are frequently the result of stereotypes, lack of contact with specific groups, and lowered confidence at being able to relate to people of difference.

Even though men and women spend a lot of time together in many different roles, gender differences create problems for some mentoring pairs. Some fear that sexual attraction between a male/female mentoring pair might become problematic or that a male mentor may not be able to deal with the supposed "emotionalism" of women. Mentoring across race, gender, culture, and global locations can be challenging and brings with it an opportunity to expand our understanding of differences. Participants have reported that mentoring across differences has brought about more understanding of diversity than any training received in a classroom. More information can be found on this subject by reviewing the presentations and publication on *Cross-Cultural Mentoring: Dialogues that Create Inclusion* (Boags, 2008).

Differences across a corporate culture can be just as challenging to mentoring partners. Mentoring across professions, business lines, departments, subsidiaries, regional locations and corporate functions requires the participants to broaden their understanding of business practices in other areas. By standing in another's shoes and seeing the world from a different perspective, we naturally expand our view of a business enterprise. This form of mentoring is especially fruitful in executive mentoring programs. Very powerful bonds and learning have occurred when peers have mentored one another in companies that have merged. The mentee coming from the acquired company needs to learn not only new operational procedures, but the culture and special language of the acquiring company.

The same holds true for workers who immigrate to this country, especially when English is not their native language. For some employees in this circumstance, mentoring has been a savior in helping them to get a firmer grip on American culture, regional differences, and specific nuances of the language. One high-level scientist in a research laboratory had emigrated from an Eastern European country. For years, he had been laughing at jokes because his co-workers laughed. He did it without knowing what the jokes meant. With a mentor, he could ask for a translation without feeling stupid. The scientist later discovered that some of the jokes weren't very funny after all and he no longer felt compelled to laugh along with his co-workers.

C. Other People: Bosses, Peers, Spouses, etc.

For years, potential mentoring partners have worried about the attitudes and opinions of one's immediate boss, super-visor, and manager. That's one reason the formal programs usually match mentoring pairs outside of a mentee's direct line of reporting. If you are searching for a mentoring partner on your own, you might also consider this strategy. I think it's a wise choice. One reason is that bosses sometimes get curious and jealous. They may worry about what's being said about them. Some mentoring pairs are concerned that the advice given by a mentor may conflict with directions given by the mentee's immediate supervisor. Such a potential conflict could become a cause for concern and ultimately the mentee must make a choice.

An aspiring writer applied for and received a fellowship to a summer institute. She very much wanted to take the time off and attend. The institute was a part of her long-range career plan, which did not include staying with her current employer. Her immediate boss could not see the importance of the move and its relevance to her current position, so he denied the leave request. Her mentor, on the other hand, saw the institute as a part of a larger context—her career path for the next five years. It was a demonstration of the perspective of boss vs. a mentor. Bosses look for immediate results, and mentors can look broadly and extend their vision into the future. In the end, each mentee must make a decision about which path to follow, as this mentee did and attended the institute. After all, each employee, whether a mentee or not, owns **their** own career.

Peers in one's immediate work environment can sometimes be pesky, inquisitive, and demoralizing. Depending upon the level of the mentee, peers sometimes see a co-worker being mentored as "breaking ranks." They see the mentee in a mentoring partnership wanting more than what's available locally and striving to expand. Take heart; once you leave for that better job and better pay, you won't have to listen to negative comments about your mentoring experience.

Spouses and other family members need to be informed about the importance of the mentoring partnership. You can keep down a lot of unnecessary friction and worry by bringing them into the mentoring circle. Some mentoring partners have come up with very creative ways for handling potential conflicts and jealousies. One female mentee invited her male mentor to dinner so that her husband could meet him. After a few such meetings, the mentor ended up advising both of them.

D. Distance, Time, and Location

Successful mentoring matches do occur between people who live in different geographic locations and time zones. Scheduling can be difficult if both parties travel a lot. Some mentoring pairs have elected to meet outside of their work day, either after or before. People who are committed know that they must accommodate each other's schedules and make the meeting times and contact points work for both of them.

A lack of time is an element that many say is one of the biggest barriers to successful mentoring. With good planning, many mentoring pairs spend as little as two hours a month in their mentoring discussions and make the time count. A big part of their success rests upon regularly scheduled meetings and an agenda for each meeting. Finding time isn't that hard either. Many mentoring pairs working at the same location schedule a long lunch together once or twice a month. This block of time has been found to be the most convenient meeting time for many mentoring pairs.

SECTION 7
YOUR PATH FORWARD

What are your next steps? It would be my wish that whether you have designated yourself as a mentor or mentee-or both- you have obtained enough information to get started on a mentoring partnership or enhance a current one. Hopefully, I have added enough additional resources so that you can satisfy yourself that the decisions you make regarding mentorship are the right ones for you.

My closing remarks for mentees:

For those who have decided to start on their mentorship journey – Start today. It's in your hands now. Remember you own your career. Once you have identified what you need to work on and where you want to go in your career, you can start the search. Use the tools that are provided in the Appendix Section and the Resources listed in this book. Your employer may offer generous benefits for career enhancements in the way of educational reimbursement and career develop-ment workshops. Take advantage of them. Look around you. Notice the people who are at the top of their game. Talk to people you work with. Seek to do better. Be pro-active. Make yourself a magnet to attract mentors.

For those already in a mentoring partnership, you can enhance and enrich what you currently have. If you already have a mentor that you're happy with, perhaps you can add another one. Expand and enlarge your comfort zone by going across gender, cultural and organizational boundaries. Learn more about your current position, the company or agency you are working in. Consider peer mentoring. Reach out to counterparts across divisions, departments or regional areas.

If you have been with your present employer or current profession for 5 to 10 years, it's time to start mentoring others. You might want to begin with the new hires or newcomers into your division or work area.

A few thoughts for mentors:

For those readers who belong to the more experienced group of employees, especially the soon-to-depart Baby Boomers, there are a lot of people who need you. Look back over your years of experience and make a list of the top 10 things that you have learned. There are people around you who could benefit from what you know. It is easy to take these lessons for granted because you rely on this information every day. What you have acquired in your personal storehouse of wisdom is specific to your industry, profession, the various roles you have held for your employers and how you have lived your life. This information can't be found anywhere else except through a dialogue with you. You can be a big asset to someone coming up through the ranks. With your input, they don't have to start over to move into your spot or something similar.

If you don't feel ready to reach out to individuals around you in the workplace, sign up for your company's mentoring program. If there is no program where you work, you may get help from your Human Resources and Training staff to facilitate a group mentoring program or small group tutorial. Reach out to your colleagues. Talk to those who are involved in mentoring whether it is formal or informal and learn how they do it.

For those who are already in a mentoring partnership, I say Bravo to you. Can you make it a deeper or richer experience? Can you engage in shadow mentoring by taking your mentees through a typical day with you, or invite them to attend meetings or conferences or accompany you on a sales call? Can you add someone else to your list? Can you stretch yourself and make yourself available for a cross-cultural or cross-company match?

There are so many possibilities for dialogue awaiting all of us. Let's move forward and make it happen. Continue to sharpen your skills. Participate in the mentoring webinars and workshop summits in your area. Above all, stay in touch. Visit my websites and let me know how you're doing.

SECTION 8
EPILOGUE

Setting up a program of your own

The kind of program that I suggest you set up for yourself if you are independently employed or for co-workers where there is no mentoring program is similar to a study group or Master-Mind group (Vitale & Hibbler, 2006). In each case, a small group of people, usually eight to twelve, meets on a regular basis to discuss issues that are relevant to the group. At times, these are strictly peer meetings; at other times, a subject matter expert (SME) is invited to attend the meetings and share his or her expertise with the group. I recommend that you seek to establish the latter. Here's how this has worked in other organizations.

Starting with a Support (Affinity) Group

A women's support group wanted to establish a mentoring program for the women in their Leadership Development Program. They were told that no funds were available and that this was something they should do on their own, so they did. With the encouragement of one of the instructors of the program (the author), they met every month at noon so that no time off could be counted against them. Each month, they invited a senior-level executive or a senior scientist to visit with them and share knowledge and career information. This format was so successful that several of the SMEs started to suggest other colleagues to invite and took it upon themselves to extend the invitation. The group wanted to expand and have an afternoon of panel discussions. One of the SMEs arranged this as an official training workshop. Through the discussions and later contact with the SMEs, many of the women found individual mentors.

Mentoring Roundtables

When organizations do not want to invest in setting up and administering a formal mentoring program, they frequently try to mimic the informal mentoring that exists in every organization. This effort to mimic informal mentoring sometimes takes the form of inviting prospective mentees and mentors to a luncheon or other gathering, having a speaker, and then expecting the attendees to mingle and have the right mentoring partners find each other. This approach almost universally fails. A way to help potential mentoring pairs find one another is to invite mentees and prospective mentors to attend a series of roundtable discussions based upon content and function. Each roundtable consists of a single profession or function. A panel of three to four prospective mentors and a facilitator lead the roundtable, which lasts for approximately forty-five minutes each. Mentees choose to sit at a roundtable based upon their interest. They elect to continue the discussion after the event with whomever strikes their interest.

Some professional associations have introduced the roundtable idea at their conferences so that possible matches can be made with attendess from a broad spectrum of businesses, industries and government agencies. The roundtable idea is also a great way for program coordinators to share best practices in the design and implementation of their programs.

Group Mentoring with Rotating Mentors

In a cross between the first and the second formats, a group mentoring experience can be formed. This involves a group of employees who have a specific core of interests and invite a small number of mentors (SMEs) to attend their meetings for several sessions. Once a topic is adequately covered, the participants can choose a new topic and invite a different set of mentors. Or the mentee group can break up and reform itself into a new group which invites a different group of experts to conduct discussion on another set of topics. Any number of groups can be formed with different sets of mentors. These discussion series are open-ended and are conducted as long as a group is willing to form and spend their time in this dynamic form of professional exchange. Over the course of a year, the participants are exposed to a large number of experts and members of management within an organization and many find suitable individual mentors as well.

One of the downsides of group mentoring is the lack of confidentiality that exists in a group, so the sessions appear more like tutorials rather than the traditional one-on-one mentoring. Even so, the information that mentees acquire and the ability to ask pertinent questions of managers and SMEs far outweighs the downside. Besides, many mentees have met a prospective mentor in this way. Mentors also gain by learning what some of the issues are for specific groups; i.e., women, minority groups, dual-career families, etc. When a person learns in this direct manner, he or she is less likely to assume that life in the organization is the same for everyone.

SECTION 9
APPENDIX

APPENDIX

Career Guidance Worksheets

PRESENT PERFORMANCE ISSUES	
Accountabilities	**List the major accountabilities of your present job.** You may want to double-check these with your immediate supervisor.
Competencies	**What Competencies are needed for mastering your present job?**
	How do your competencies stack up in terms of your present accountabilities?
	Where are your strengths?
	Where are your areas of needed growth?
NOTES	

PRESENT PERFORMANCE ISSUES Cont'd	
Areas of Development	**Personal** (technical, educational, etc.)
	Interpersonal (relationship issues between you and other key persons – both in the workplace and outside it.)
	Organizational (links between you and the organization; your job and the business, etc.)
Developmental Activities and Action Items	**List those developmental activities that you have started or plan to start in the near future.**
NOTES	

Mentorship: A Pathway to Career Success

CAREER GOALS	
Long-Term Career Objectives	**Position Objectives:** What is your ideal or optimum position?
	Options: What are some alternatives to the ideal or optimum?
	Competencies needed for the optimum position?
	Present capabilities, knowledge and experiences available for the desired position:
NOTES	

CAREER GOALS Cont'd	
Near Term Position Objectives	**Next Career Move**: Ideally where would you like to move in order to be in a better position to achieve your optimum position?
	Options: What might be a suitable alternative if you cannot find your ideal next move?
	Competencies needed for the position you have identified:
	Capabilities, knowledge and experiences presently available for the identified position:
Gaps	**Areas of development identified**:
Resources	**People who could help me**:

APPENDIX B

The Mentoring Plan Summary

The Mentoring Plan Summary

As Mentor and Mentee in a learning partnership, we have discussed our future agenda and decided to meet a minimum of_____times per _____. We both understand that the minimum required meeting time is once per month for the next _____months. During these meetings we have decided to discuss the issues as listed below.

As we proceed through our mutually agreed-upon agenda, we will alter this plan as needed, adding or deleting topics as appropriate. We also agree to keep an informal journal of our discussion topics and the challenges that arise during our meetings. This will help us evaluate our progress during our periodic follow-up and evaluation sessions.

The following general topics have been chosen for our discussion during our initial mentoring meetings:

1.OUR GOALS FOR THE PARTNERSHIP

2. OUR EXPECTATIONS

3. OBSTACLES WE FORESEE

4. METHODS TO OVERCOME THE OBSTACLES

Mentorship: A Pathway to Career Success

5.MENTEE DISCUSSION ITEMS

6. MENTOR DISCUSSION ITEMS

7. PROGRESS EVALUATION AND UPDATES

Please continue and complete the next sheet of the Summary.

The Mentoring Plan Summary

Ground Rules for Managing the Partnership

By mutual agreement the following ground rules have been established to govern the management of our partnership. These ground rules will establish certain responsibilities to be carried out regarding our meeting times, meeting content, negotiating activities together, settling conflicts, and any other issues which are of importance to us. The first three items are suggested for all partnerships.

1. Confidentiality

_____

_____

2. Integrity

_____

_____

3. Commitment

_____

_____

4. _____

_____

5. _____

_____

Use additional sheets or reverse side if necessary to complete the Agreement.

Signature_____Date_____
                  Mentee

Signature_____Date_____
                  Mentor

APPENDIX **C**

Mentoring Readiness Questionnaires

Mentee Readiness Self-Assessment

Am I Ready to be a Mentee?

Use the answers to this section, and the thinking that goes into your choices, to help you decide if you are ready to make a commitment to mentoring. There are no right or wrong answers to the questions below. On the whole, a majority of YES answers indicates that you are ready to participate in a Mentoring Partnership. Indicate your readiness by putting a check mark (Y) in the appropriate space.

		YES	NO
1.	I want to take more responsibility for my own career progress.	☐	☐
2.	I want to explore other parts of the company.	☐	☐
3.	I want to assess career goals relative to work-life balance	☐	☐
4.	I want to further develop my discipline and/or functional skill base.	☐	☐
5.	I want to know if I have the right skills to achieve my career goals, and if not, what new skills I need.	☐	☐
6.	I want information about where we are going as a company.	☐	☐
7.	I want to increase my exposure to people that I don't normally interact with	☐	☐
8.	I am ready to make the time commitment to participate in a mentoring partnership.	☐	☐
9.	I feel that understanding our organization's business strategies would help me make a greater contribution.	☐	☐
10.	I believe mentoring will make me a more valuable employee.	☐	☐

Other ways that I might benefit form a Mentoring Partnership:

_____

_____

_____

_____

_____

_____

Mentorship: A Pathway to Career Success

Mentor Readiness Self-Assessment

Am I Ready to be a Mentor?

Use the answers to this section, and the thinking that goes into your choices, to help you decide if you are ready to make a commitment to mentoring. On the whole, a majority of YES answers indicates that you are ready to participate in a mentoring partnership. Indicate your readiness by putting a check mark (Y) in the appropriate space.

		YES	NO
1.	I have the desire to help others who want to grow and develop	☐	☐
2.	I have valuable knowledge that I would like to transfer to others.	☐	☐
3.	I had a mentor early in my career and would like to "reciprocate" by mentoring others	☐	☐
4.	I would value the opportunity to develop and practice my communication and my coaching skills in a one-to-one setting.	☐	☐
5.	I would like the opportunity to get to know someone in this company who is of another race or culture	☐	☐
6.	I welcome the opportunity to be part of developing company talent.	☐	☐
7.	I am ready to make the time commitment to participate in a mentoring partnership.	☐	☐
8.	I believe in the philosophies of our business strategy and feel that the mentoring program will support our business objectives.	☐	☐
9.	I believe that mentoring will make this a better place to work.	☐	☐
10.	I believe that a mentoring partnership will make me a more valuable employee.	☐	☐

Other ways that I might benefit from a Mentoring partnership:

_____

_____

_____

_____

_____

_____

D. *Answer to a Question*

<u>**WHAT'S IT LIKE TO HAVE A MENTOR?**</u>
<u>**By Rita S. Boags, Ph.D.**</u>

1. HAVING A MENTOR IS LIKE HAVING A PIPELINE TO BURIED TREASURE.

- That buried treasure is the knowledge and wisdom that the person has accumulate throughout their life and career
- It's tapping into their experience and learning
- It's reaping the benefits from their problems and solutions
- It's seeing what possible from the challenges that they have faced and overcome

2. HAVING A MENTOR IS PUTTING YOURSELF IN THE ROLE OF STUDENT AGAIN.

IT'S BEING ABLE TO SAY OPENLY AND HONESTLY...

- There are things that I don't know or know how to do
- I don't have all the answers
- There are things I want to be taught
- I want to learn and grow

3. HAVING A MENTOR IS OPENING YOURSELF TO THINGS YOU MAY NOT WANT TO KNOW-ESPECIALLY ABOUT YOURSELF.

4. HAVING A MENTOR IS LIKE HAVING A MIRROR THAT TALKS TO YOU.

5. HAVING A MENTORING RELATIONSHIP IS A PRECIOUS COMMODITY...

- That requires care and nurturing and
- Must be held in high regard

6. HAVING A MENTOR IS LIKE HAVING A GUIDE...

- Who can point out the potholes along the path
- Who can help you find the quickest and best route to your goals

7. HAVING A MENTOR IS LIKE HAVING ANOTHER...

- Pair of eyes to see with
- Brain to think with
- Another life to add to your own

8. HAVING A MENTOR OFFERS THE PROSPECT OF GREATER MATURITY.

- You get to respect another human being, warts and all
- You learn to accept both smallness and greatness

9. HAVING A MENTOR IS LIKE HAVING A MID-WIFE WHO ASSISTS YOU IN THE BIRTH OF A NEW YOU.

- Since we are all constantly evolving and developing or dying.

10. HAVING A MENTOR IS LIKE HAVING AN X-RAY BEAMED ON YOUR LIFE AND CAREER.

11. HAVING A MENTOR MEANS TAKING RISKS IN COMMUNICATING NEW IDEAS AND EXPRESSING ONE'S INNER SELF.

12. HAVING A MENTOR IS HAVING ANOTHER PERSON IN THE WORLD CARE ABOUT YOU, YOUR CAREER, AND ULTIMATELY YOUR LIFE.

SECTION 10
RESOURCES

References

Abbott, I.O. and R.S. Boags (2003). *Mentoring Across Differences: A Guide to Cross-Race and Cross-Gender Mentoring Partnerships.* Available from Minority Corporate Counsel Association, New York. Download free at *www.mcca.com/site/data/researchprograms/GoldPathways/index.shtml*

Anderson, J. (2007) "Morgan Stanley to Settle Sex Bias Suit," *New York Times*, April 25, C1.

Bixler, S. (1991) *Professional Presence*. New York: G.P.Putnam & Sons.

Boags, R.S. (2007) *Are You Ready for 2010?* Webinar presentation available for download at *www.leadershiptechnologies.com*.

_____. (2008) *Cross-Cultural Mentoring: Dialogues that Create Inclusion*. Castro Valley, CA:Leadership Technologies.

_____. (2006) *Fixing the Ten Most Common Mistakes of Formal Mentoring Programs*. Webinar presentation available for download at *www.leadershiptechnologies.com*.

_____. (2005) *Mentoring: A Core Strategy for Inclusion and Equity*. Article available for download at *www.leadershiptechnolgies.com*.

_____. (2003) *The Mentoring Bridge: A Self-Management Guide to Informal Mentoring Partnerships.* Castro Valley, CA: Leadership Technologies.

_____. (2004) *Strategies for Building a Diverse Leadership Pipeline.* White paper available for download at *www.leadershiptechnolgies. com.*

_____. (2002) *Implementing a Best Practices Mentoring Program: Coordinator's Guide and Toolkit.* Castro Valley, CA: Leadership Technologies.

_____. *(2002) MENTORING: Information Guide.* Castro Valley, CA: Leadership Technologies.

_____. (2002) *Mentoring Partnership Workshop-Introduction to Mentoring and Advanced Mentoring Workshop.* Castro Valley, CA: Leadership Technologies.

Boyle, M. (2005) "Most Mentoring Programs Stink – but yours doesn't have to." *Training* magazine, August, pp. 12–15.

Cottrell, D. (2002) *Monday Morning Leadership: 8 Mentoring Sessions You Can't Afford to Miss.* Dallas, TX: Cornerstone Leadership Institute.

Fornal, P. and D. Sanchez. (2005) SHRM White Paper "Employee Engagement and Organizational Performance: How do you know your employees are engaged?" Alexandria, VA: SHRM Information Center

Garfinkel, P. (2004) "Executive Life: Putting a Formal Stamp on Mentoring." *New York Times,* January 18.

Kaye, B. (2002) *Love 'Em or Lose 'Em: Getting Good People to Stay.* San Francisco: Berrett-Koeler.

Lavelle, L. (2004) "MANAGEMENT: How To Groom The Next Boss" *BusinessWeek,* April 19.

Mentoring Application and Tracking System (MATS™). Go to *www. mentoringanalysis.com* for a description of the program.

Scheele, A. (1983) *Skills for Success – A Guide to the Top for Men and Women.* New York: Ballantine Books.

The Conference Board. (2005) *Managing the Mature Workforce.* New York

Vitale, J. and B. Hibbler. (2006) *Meet & Grow Rich. How to Easily Create and Operate Your Own "Mastermind" Group for Health, Wealth, and More.* Hoboken, NJ: John Wiley & Sons.

Waterman, R.H., J.A. Waterman, and B.A. Collard. (1994) "Toward a Career Resilient Workforce." *Harvard Business Review,* July-August, pp. 87–95.

Zey, M.G. (1995) *The Mentor Connection: Strategic Alliances in Corporate Life.* New Brunswick, NJ: Transaction Publishers.

Leadership Technologies' Mentoring Products and Services

☐ **Coordinator's Guide and Toolkit:**
IMPLEMENTING A BEST PRACTICES MENTORING INITIATIVE

The essential features of the Coordinator's Guide are the 14 Key Elements which define a *Best Practices* program. The 14 Key Elements are divided into Four Phases for ease of program implementation. These phases provide an end-to-end roadmap for the initiation and completion of a Mentoring Program. Available online in an E-Format, hard copy or CD.

Special Toolkit Features
- Design flowcharts, templates and forms
- Sample presentations, letters and announcements
- Brochure and Booklet Templates
- Questionnaires for measuring program readiness and participant progress
- ✧ Take the Coordinator's Guide tour at www.mentoringanalysis.com

☐ **MENTORING: Information Guide**

A user-friendly primer on Mentoring for all levels in an organization. It is designed for all audiences including: Mentors, Mentees (Proteges) Managers, Coordinator, Program team members, and sponsors.

Primarily used during the Initial phase of a program implementation to inform and educate the applicant population on the topic of Mentoring and help to dispel common myths and misconceptions.

☐ **Mentoring Partnership Workshop Workbooks**

The training manual for Mentor/Mentee Pairs contains the materials for two complete workshops – introductory and advanced along with a 5-part Appendix needed for starting and sustaining a successful mentoring partnership.
1) Introduction to Mentoring and
2) Cultivating the Mentoring Partnership
3) Extensive Appendix with Mentoring Partnership Tools and Resources e.g., a Learning Plan, Partnership Agreement and Mentoring Journal
✧ Facilitator's training recommended with companion workbook

☐ **Mentoring Training Videos**

Presents 3 case studies of the common challenges facing mentoring partnerships as they begin their Mentoring journey. The case study characters represent a range of diverse populations. Each case study includes a problem statement, resolution, discussion topics and a summary of key teaching points at the end of each case.

✧ Used in conjunction with the Mentoring Partnership Workshop or as a stand-alone training.
✧ Includes Facilitator's Manual and PPT overheads Template
✧ For a more complete description, go online to the publisher's site at www.leadershiptechnologies.com/Products

Leadership Technologies' Mentoring Products and Services

☐ Manager's Mentoring Guide

This companion guide is designed for the Managers of Mentees and is frequently used as a handout during Management Briefings. The guide explains the mentoring process used in the sponsoring organization and clarifies the Manager's Role in the mentoring program.
◇ Customization, volume discounts and self-publishing available

☐ The Mentoring Bridge: A Self-Management Guide to Informal Mentoring Partnerships

A do-it-yourself guide to mentoring partnerships. This Guide is a comprehensive workbook for those not involved in a formal mentoring program and who wish to start a partnership on their own. A step-by-step roadmap suitable for Mentees and Mentors at any level. Contains an extensive Appendix with self-assessments, planning documents and journal template.

This fully illustrated workbook is used in the Mentoring Bridge Workshop and Development Program
◇ Volume pricing and self-publishing available

☐ Mentoring Application and Tracking System (MATS™)

Online Mentoring Administrative Tool - Used by mentoring programs to
♦ Collect mentor and mentee applicant data
  • Create mentoring profiles for applicants
  • Manage mentor and mentee applicant pool
♦ Facilitate Matching - assists mentees in finding best mentor matches
♦ Monitor the status of mentoring partnerships
  • Partnership goal-setting documents
  • Mentoring Evaluations - Periodic checkpoint questionnaires
  • Event attendance
♦ Can be customized for each client

☐ Mentoring Interest Survey

Assess your organization's readiness for mentoring
Does your company need a mentoring program? Are certain groups the recipients of informal mentoring and others not? What myths and misconceptions are holding your employees back from forming mentoring partnerships on their own? Find out the answers to these and other key questions before you start a mentoring program. A Free trial of this questionnaire is available at www.mentoringanalysis.com

☐ Mentoring Website Template

Every program must have a website for informing potential participants, educating the workforce, collecting applications and answering inquiries. Find out more about how this template can ease the burden of creating a web-site from nothing. Generous content is based upon the popular educational tool, *MENTORING: Information Guide.*
◇ For a more complete description visit www.mentoringanalysis.com

For more details, pricing and ordering information go to www.leadershiptechnologies.com

Leadership Technologies' Mentoring Products and Services

☐ **Webinars and Workshops on Demand**

A series of webinars and public workshops are offered throughout the year on a variety of subjects ranging from how to avoid mistakes in setting up mentoring programs, to cross-cultural mentoring, deconstructing the Glass Ceiling and much more. See topic list below:

- *Mentoring Fundamentals: Successful Program Design*
- *Mentoring across Differences: Dialogues that Create Inclusion*
- *Creating a Diverse Leadership Pipeline*
- *Build an Inclusive Culture with Multiple Mentoring Formats*
- *Managing and Mentoring Diverse Talent*

Visit our Website at www.leadershiptechnologies.com to schedule a topic.

Printed in the United States
126508LV00002B/1-108/P